Martha's Prayer Book
When Busyness is Next to Godliness

40 Days of Conversations with God

Betty Murphy

Parson's Porch Books

www.parsonsporchbooks.com

Martha's Prayer Book: When Busyness is Next to Godliness
ISBN: Softcover 978-1-949888-62-1
Copyright © 2019 by Betty Murphy

All rights reserved. No part of this book may be reproduced or transmitted in any form or by any means, electronic or mechanical, including photocopying, recording, or by any information storage and retrieval system, without permission in writing from the publisher.

Table of Contents

Preface	1
Part I: Supplication	3
Beginning	5
Spending	6
Reading	7
Singing	8
Rebooting	9
Persevering	10
Respecting	11
Enduring	12
Adjusting	13
Redeeming	14
Encouraging	15
Missing	16
Accepting	17
Stressing	18
Caring	19
Serving	20
Tiring	21
Progressing	22
Rebuilding	23
Trusting	24
Prioritizing	27
Surviving	28
Acquiescing	29
Interceding	30
Admiring	31
Hoping	32
Expecting	33
Despairing	34
Remembering	35
Valuing	36
Cleaning	37
Tolerating	38
Constructing	39
Welcoming	40
Providing	41
Empathizing	42
Searching	43
Embarking	44
Part II: Meditation	45
Beginning	47
Spending	47
Reading	47
Singing	47
Rebooting	47
Persevering	47
Respecting	48
Enduring	48
Adjusting	48
Redeeming	48
Encouraging	48
Missing	48
Accepting	49
Stressing	49
Caring	49
Serving	49
Tiring	49
Progressing	49
Rebuilding	50
Trusting	50
Appreciating	50
Concurring	50
Prioritizing	50
Surviving	50
Acquiescing	51
Interceding	51
Admiring	51
Hoping	51
Expecting	51
Despairing	51
Remembering	51
Valuing	52

Cleaning	52	Progressing	71
Tolerating	52	Rebuilding	72
Constructing	52	Trusting	73
Welcoming	52	Appreciating	74
Providing	52	Concurring	75
Empathizing	53	Prioritizing	76
Searching	53	Surviving	77
Embarking	53	Acquiescing	78
Part III: Application	**54**	Interceding	79
Beginning	57	Admiring	80
Spending	57	Hoping	81
Singing and Reading	58	Remembering	82
Rebooting	59	Valuing	83
Respecting	60	Cleaning	84
Persevering	61	Tolerating	85
Enduring	62	Constructing	86
Adjusting	63	Welcoming	87
Redeeming	64	Providing	88
Encouraging	65	Empathizing	89
Missing	65	Searching	90
Accepting	66	Embarking	91
Stressing	67		
Caring	68		
Serving	69		
Tiring	70		

Preface

I was watching a live-stream video of a little church I used to attend. True to its philosophy of using every member, the leadership had tapped an elderly parishioner to conduct the offertory prayer. It was brief, focused, and incredibly sweet. Her message was couched in the Elizabethan diction of the King James Bible, words that might sound strange to a contemporary ear. There was no mistaking, however, this dear lady's relationship to the Almighty. He heard, and worshippers were blessed by her simple expression of gratitude.

Prayer is simply connecting with Someone Who is always on call. He wants to be included in our busy lives and is truly gracious when we ask Him to participate. The pages that follow are meant to illustrate the random, desperate need to take the chaos of everyday living into His presence. Even if our requests come from "out in left field," we'll find Him there at home plate, waving us on.

I've found the most effective prayer in my repertoire is also the simplest: *Help!*

Martha's Prayer Book is intended to be enjoyed as an encouraging volume showing that conversations with God can be humorous, unconventional, brutally honest or inconclusive. Topical scriptures have been added for *Reflection*, along with life style *Applications* for further consideration. Since *Marthas* are busy people, they should decide the best way to use this little collection of inspiration. It is meant to be a guilt-free product. In a pinch, it's a great doorstop!

Betty Murphy

2019

Part I: Supplication

Life is hard, but prayer isn't.
God is saying,
"Tell Me how you really feel!"

Beginning

Here I am, Lord, keeping that New Year's resolution—the one about having a "quiet time." I'm tired of being the bad guy in the story, the one who is always worried about many things and didn't make the better choice. I know all the reasons I should be here, all the time worn slogans like this one:

If you don't come apart, you will come apart.

I know Martin Luther felt a busy day should start
with three hours of prayer.

I know You said we should *pray without ceasing.*

I'm trying to unclench my fists and lay my neglect driven guilt at Your feet.

Help me forget about the piles of decorations to put away…

> The baskets of dirty laundry,
>
> The sticky pie plates,
>
> The trash, overflowing with gift wrap,
>
> The piles of waiting paperwork,
>
> The demands of the work week,
>
> The extra pounds that urgently require an exercise routine.

I'm coming apart, all right!

Please help me; I'm not good at this "sitting at your feet" thing.

You spoke the world into being, calmed the sea, withered an unproductive tree—all with a word.

I don't have that kind of clout.

Even so, I'm going to take a deep breath
and ask You to speak again—

to this yawning, unkempt, unprofitable servant
Who wants to seek you first in this new year.

Lord, have mercy on me, a Martha.

Spending

Lord, I can tell from the junk mail that January sales are in full swing. That is one perk of constant busyness —not a minute for shopping. It's time-consuming enough just to haul all the coupon books and newsprint "deals" to the recycle bin. I'm still trying to find room for the unwrapped gifts piled in the family room. I think we "over-consumed" again.

I wonder if You cringe at the way we celebrate Your birthday.
I have many questions about the spending habits of good stewards.
I know about the tithe.
I read that you love a cheerful giver.
I'm aware that we reap what we sow.
I remember we must help widows and orphans.
Somehow none of those principles help me a whole lot.

Every Christian ministry is pleading for a donation with a matching gift. Every organization is collecting for a legitimate need. The church is soliciting for the building fund.
There are so many "worthy causes" my head spins.

I'm aware of the victims of the year's disasters.
I know somewhere children are dying of malnutrition.
I am bombarded with requests for research money
for harmful diseases.

Then along comes Christmas…

Is it wrong to buy new X-Boxes and expensive jeans with pre-made holes in the knees?

Isn't the old sofa good enough?

And a present exchange at the Bible Study—
couldn't we just focus on the Greatest Gift?

Lord, I would give anything to watch You stroll the streets of modern America.

Please walk beside me this year and show me the best way to use the generous resources you've given.

Reading

Oh Lord, the temptation of it all! I'm going to weigh 400 pounds.

At home, at work, at a stop between errands, it's the ultimate treat: lunch and a good book.

Two new gift reads sit near the breakfast table. Another has just shipped. Devices deliver fact and fiction at the stroke of a fingertip. My bookshelves runneth over

Having earned the right to a break, I scrape the soup bowl, pursue every crumb, chase down every grain of rice in the diet meal—just so I can turn another page. This simple pleasure is the highlight of my day.

Thank You, Lord, for the power of communication. Thank You for fantasies, and ideas, and mystery, and humor, and advice, and history, and adventure.

Help me in the choices of words I allow to flow through my mind. Show me how to revel in the Book of Books.

Teach me about the beauty of holiness as I sing the Psalms and absorb the wisdom of Solomon.

Guide me by the example of the Israelites crossing the pages of scripture.

Exhort me with the instruction of the Apostles.

I love the way you are described as The Word. When I pore over the pages of Holy Writ, there You are, living and breathing, walking on the water, healing troubled minds and bodies.

Because Your presence enhances every activity of my day, be pleased to look over my shoulder and guide my thoughts as I enjoy the miraculous impact of the printed page. Join me wherever I am transported and teach me the way to find lessons in the assortment of characters who follow the author's plot to its resolution.

Lord, show me the story line You have for me. Help me to stick to the *Plan* and be a blessing to the other characters I meet along the way.

Singing

When I heard the cruel order, my heart sank for the people under the control of the harsh dictator. Music is now illegal in his country. One news feed indicated the people were no longer allowed to smile as well. Doesn't that go without saying? If I had no music, I wouldn't be smiling either.

Lord, how I pray for those starving, oppressed, disconsolate people. Their bodies are always in danger; now an evil ruler seeks to starve their souls. Give them melodies in their hearts, Oh God. Send a thousand birds to sing Your carols. Let every bubbling spring, every whispering breeze, and every insect drone declare the glory of the Creator whose love cannot be quenched by many waters.

Thank You for allowing us the freedom to give voice to our rejoicing.

…..for all those versions of *Amazing Grace* and *Jesus Loves me*

…..for the *Hallelujah Chorus*

…..for the classic hymns of the faith

…..and toe tapping gospel

…..and *Gregorian Chants*

…..and *Joy to the World* carols

……and *Easter Alleluias*

…..and *organ concertos*

…..and *contemporary Christian*, even the songs with *"whoa, whoa, whoa's"*

May we always rejoice that our citizenship is in heaven by singing praises to the One who purchased our passport there!

Lord, we know the morning stars sang as you created the universe. Even then, You knew we'd be teaching our toddlers "Twinkle, Twinkle, Little Star"

And glorying in Your gift of song.

Rebooting

Why are they changing the computer programs again?

We've barely learned the last ones. Everyone is out in the halls, Lord, saying the same thing, "Does anybody know how to…" It's a real catalyst for getting people to work together.

I'm sorry for berating the IT person. No, she didn't present the new stuff well. Couldn't she give us a written guide, just in case we didn't understand her hundred mile an hour explanation? Still, it was really ugly of me to tell her I was going to toss my computer out the window.

I hope these changes were really necessary. Someone said there were bugs in the system. I'm always suspicious of these techies. They're continually on the trail of every innovation that comes down the pike. Nobody's going to be *sharing documents*; they're just going to walk across the hall! And virtual sticky notes? Give me a break! How do you throw your gum away in one of those?

Lord, I'll bet You're about to jump all over my case. Take my bad attitude, for starters. I suspect you've always been on the side of the techies anyway. Now that I have made you my Default, You're forever making changes to my programs too. My system has plenty of "bugs" all right, but what's a few bugs between friends?

I know when you want me to upgrade, You aren't asking anything from me that You didn't accomplish Yourself. When You were still a young boy, You grew in wisdom and in favor with God and man. Even though You were the Son of God, You didn't skip any part of the curriculum.

I'm not sure I can even hope to be like Paul. He knew he had not attained the goals set before him, but he pressed on. He had pretty big aspirations, didn't he? Knowing You, and the power of Your resurrection, even the fellowship of Your suffering were high on his list. That makes learning a new computer program seem pretty tame.

OK, Lord, I'll apologize to the Tech and give the new software another shot. But I'm going to need Your help!

Persevering

Lord, forgive my misinterpretation, but when I read the words of Matthew 24 about the days being cut short for the sake of your chosen ones, I can only think of February.

Trees are dark skeletons against the monochromatic drab of the sky, but I can appreciate a little stark beauty. The utter gloom is another issue. I don't find gray anywhere in the rainbow.

By February we have quit going to the gym, neglected our Bibles, and lost our enthusiasm for a new start. We look to a Pennsylvania groundhog for the promise of spring, while raking the snow off the windshield.

February is not just a month. It can also be a season of our lives, beginning in those "no light at the end of the tunnel" moments.

Life seems meaningless, even in Its hopeless busyness.
The days drag endlessly by.

"Same old/same old" is our watchword.
Some of us have to get on with life.
Some of us have no life to get on with.

Lord, remind me of Your antidote for the dark times:
Malachi wrote of the "Sun of Righteousness"
Who will rise with rays of healing in His wings,
And talked of the promise that we will
frolic like calves let out of the barn.

A pinpoint of light is easy to see in the darkness.
Sometimes, however, we can miss it in the gray gloom.
Don't let me do that, Lord.

I know the pilot light in my gas fireplace is always on.
With the flick of a switch, I can produce radiant heat,
Unless the battery's dead or the igniter doesn't work.

Ignite my February days with the reminder:
"I know that my Redeemer lives!"
And let that be enough.

Respecting

I can hardly bear to face the headlines these days, Lord. What has happened to our country? As if obvious differences aren't enough, we even hate people for their ideas.

Maybe for one day we could, no matter how grudgingly, practice elementary school kindness. Maybe we could see that everyone receives a card with a heart or two.

I remember my Fourth Grade Valentine mailbox. Like everyone else, I was responsible for its design. Unlike everyone else, I was an artistic klutz. The mail slit in the shoebox was torn and jagged; the glue made the white crepe paper transparent so everyone could clearly see the writing underneath. Even the anticipation of candy hearts could not quell the embarrassment I would feel when the monstrosity was placed on my desk the next morning.

Way back then, Lord, You looked after me. Mamma was sick, so I went home with a friend-- not just any friend, but a friend whose mother had a extra shoe box and plenty of ideas about using her spare crepe paper. I can still picture that pretty mailbox she helped me make.

I will say, Lord, I always did my best to see that no one in the class was left off my Valentine Day list. OK, I admit to sending the cards with skunks and other less than desirable critters to the yucky boys, but why would they want a fluffy kitten or a Cinderella anyway?

Wouldn't it be wonderful, Lord, if we stopped using our technology to criticize, shame, and dishonor people?

Wouldn't it be great if we gave everyone a fair shake, even those with different ideas?

Wouldn't our country be a better place if we looked for ways to express our kindness, and Yours.

Doesn't everybody deserve a valentine?

Show me Your list, and I'll see what I can do.

Enduring

Where do we go from here, Lord.
This is his third time in rehab.
Isn't there something biblical about three?

Noah had three sons;
The Ark contained three items;
Peter had three visions.
Then there are the biggies like the Trinity and your Resurrection on the third day.
I think there were three wise men,
but maybe that was just their gifts.

OK, I admit it. I'm grasping at straws, but I am so desperate to see him free from the cravings that are destroying him…and us.

Rehab isn't cheap, You know.

We've cut every corner to pay for this flimsy hope.

My stomach is always in knots. At least I'll know he's safe for a few weeks.

Then there's the guilt. What did we do wrong? He had every advantage: sports, vacations, the best schools, churches and youth groups.

His siblings feel neglected. His dad's impatiently washed his hands of the "prodigal."

I don't know where to turn, so once again I turn to You. I kneel by my bed and put my head in your lap while I cry out my heart.

I know You love him even more than I do, so much that You are willing to do the hard things to make him whole. I know you won't allow the pain he's caused to be wasted.

The others will be waiting for supper shortly, and I need to hear about their concerns too.

Thank you for listening, Lord, and for speaking to me through the scripture I learned as a child:

Come to me, all you who are weary and burdened, and I will give you rest.

This very afternoon I give him into Your care, because I am out of resources. I rejoice that Yours are endless.

Adjusting

Lord, we're moving again!

I am ready to weep,
wail,
gnash my teeth,
kick and scream,
and to point out I have to be willing to sign the deed
when we sell the house.

Haven't we done this enough?

I am so tired of goodbyes!

This is where I want to raise my kids—near friends and family. And we're going ever so far away.

I don't want to build a new life again!

Just about every meaningful Bible study
starts with the same person:
Abraham.

You asked him to head for a place that his descendants wouldn't inherit for four hundred years. He believed You, and it was "counted as righteousness" for him.

I believe You too, but I am no Abraham. I can't just fold my tent and head out of Dodge; I have to get three estimates from moving companies, keep the house picture perfect, and hope I can survive "in a land I have never known."

Yes, I remember the "moving" scriptures:

Here we have no continuing city, but we seek the one to come.

In my Father's house are many mansions.

The Lord is the One who goes before you.

Even so, I am not a happy camper.

You're going to have to help me with this one.

Redeeming

Ugh! If there's anything I dislike, it's a cocktail party, Lord.
I suppose we have to go--unless, of course,
You could let the world end before next Friday.

I'll be cold in the little black dress.

There won't be enough chairs, and I haven't worn heels since the last big holiday.

There'll be a bunch of unknowns, hugging me as if we were best friends. Truly I won't know a soul.

I'll spend the evening feigning interest in solar panels and tea cup poodles. Think of all the things I could be doing at home.

The language will make me uncomfortable.

Should the beverages be running low, it won't be necessary to turn the water into wine. I'll be drinking ginger ale.

As you can see, Lord, this is all about me.
I wonder how you felt all the times you hung out
with "publicans and sinners,"
or with anybody else for that matter.
I'm really grateful You are willing to hang out with me.

You find us valuable, don't You?
You are willing to bide Your time, looking for a chink in our hollow walls.

Shouldn't I be able to reciprocate somebody's offer of hospitality with a little kindness?

Sometimes a little glitter is all people have.
At least I could add a prayer.

You had no place to lay your head.
I'm unwilling to be uncomfortable for a few hours.

Is there some way You and I together could turn this event into a blessing?

That is—if the end of the world is not an option.

Encouraging

It was the phone call I didn't expect.

My dearest friend has cancer.

Lord, will You be the first responder as she absorbs this news?

Every test seems to show the worst possible diagnosis.
Even so, the doctors offer hope for a good outcome.

Hope comes with an array of uncomfortable side effects:
Hair loss,
Fatigue,
Stomach upset,
Discolored skin,
And major surgery.

It's safe to say her life will never be the same.

Will You stand by her side through it all?

Hold her so close she can feel Your arms around her.
Cheer her days with little things that make a difference
Give her big doses of Your peace that passes understanding.

Lift up her drooping hands, strengthen her feeble knees,
and make straight paths for her feet--
Paths that lead to healing and victory.

Show her the compassion and care
she has so often offered to others.

Guide the skilled hands that provide her treatment.

You are the Great Physician.
She will be reaching for the hem of Your garment.
Let Your healing power flow through her injured body
And make it well again.
Most of all, bless this time as she trusts in Your goodness
Allow her to mount up on wings like eagles
As she awaits the renewal of her strength in You.

Missing

The house is so silent when I open the door, Lord.

There is no soft snore or a click of nails on the floor,
No collar jingling with old tags and bells.

For a moment I wait for a wagging tail welcome
Until I remember he now lies
at the edge of the woods with the others.

How we love our pets, Lord.
Even a tiny fish in a bowl
seems to make us more of a family.

You thought of everything when You made the world.
You knew we would take pleasure in Your creatures,
And I imagine You had a ball playing around with
Ideas for snouts and tails and funny ears and fuzzy bodies,
Knowing how much we would enjoy Your work.

Thank you for the faithful old pet who taught us
so much about love and loyalty.
I'd turn around, and there he'd be, wanting nothing more
than to be near us.

What a lesson about our presence in the lives of others.
Sometimes just our being there is enough.

Give us the wisdom to be kind, non-judgmental, and friendly.
Show us the way to give love
with no strings attached.

I'll admit the packaging was a bit smelly.
He had bad breath in his old age.
His coat was dull, and his eyes watered.
It was a pain to have to hurry home and let him out.

His unconditional love was worth it all,
and I miss him, Lord.

I just wanted You to know.

Accepting

Why did I handle it so poorly
when she asked me to call her "Jim"?
The hormones were already working;
her voice cracked like that of a seventh grade boy
entering adulthood.

I had known this moment would come. I had thought about what to say but not about the aching heart that would have to process my words.

Lord, I didn't think what she was doing was OK with you,
and so I said,

"I don't feel right calling you the new name;
I don't think it would please the Lord,
and I don't think it's good for you."

All true. I had done the research. I knew what the shots were doing to her body, and had wept at the thought.

I spoke my piece, but I missed her heart.

Lord, how could I have answered so poorly? You knew what to say to the woman at the well whose coping skills were way off base. Why couldn't I do that?

I still have a lot to learn.

"I feel like crap when I'm a girl," she said.

Of course she did. I'd read her poetry. Her body and soul had been pained and disrespected.

Sometimes it's easier to fix the physical than the mental.
That was her choice.
She graduated as "Jim," and I have lost track of her now.

Lord, you know where she is, and I pray that my intercessions from that time follow her still.

Most of all I pray, <u>let me learn</u>! Give me Your heart of love and understanding.

Next time I want to do it right!

Stressing

Oh dear, Lord, I'm the last car in the preschool pickup line again.
I shouldn't have tried to squeeze in that last errand.

At least I'm here.

There he stands, just like every other little guy, looking nervous.
They are all like soldiers in a row, hands between their legs, as if
there is some security in clutching their manhood.

The girls are twisty and chatty, socializing and tending their baby dolls.
They seem carefree in their pink coats and sparkly boots.
Not the boys.

I wonder what so preoccupies young men at this age.
Is it just the fear of being left standing at the curb?

Do they remember they have to keep trying
until they can ride their bikes without training wheels.?

Are they thinking about the little league basketball team where they
have yet to make a basket?
Are they wondering if their *blankies* are still in their backpacks?

Only a short time ago they were ripping and running on the
playground. Tag is an easy game to play.

Their folders hold papers with teacher stickers
applauding their efforts to make a copy of the letter "J" perfectly
formed with their fat pencils.

A snack and a short stint of cartoons will soon erase the cares of the
day. Now they are solemn and big eyed, unashamed of needing their
mommies.

Sometimes I'm like a preschool boy, Lord,
Waiting to see if you'll come through for me,
Hoping to find security in the comfort of Your word.
Mostly I need to know you have my situation under control.

Sometimes, though, I'll have to say.
It seems that You are waiting in the
very back of the line.

Caring

Who would be so bold, Lord, as to strike up a conversation with two perfect strangers?

Somebody You wanted us to pray for, I guess.

We had just walked out of the restaurant.

"You two seem so happy," she said, by way of introduction.

Soon she was tearfully pouring out her story.
"What do you do when your heart is breaking,
and you can't stop crying?" she asked.

Wow, Lord! Was that ever an opening to talk about You,
the Lover of our souls.

We paused and listened.

She'd never married the father of her child,
and now he was leaving her.
She'd made him her life, the sun around which she orbited.
He'd met someone new and had moved on.
The light in her life had gone out.

Remember, how we prayed for her?
We found her a Christian counselor, and she went
Once...or maybe twice, then faded from sight.

It seems she failed to get the message, Lord,
that Her Maker will be her husband
and a father to her fatherless child.

Please stick around until she realizes
how much she needs Your care.
I know she has financial issues,
and her fourth grader could use counseling
and help with math.

By her own admission, her life is "a hot mess."

I pray she'll let You take care of it all.

Serving

Ick! Today's the day I clean the bathrooms.
I'm struggling for inspiration, Lord.

Maybe I should reflect on places
that don't have running water,
or don't have water at all,
and be grateful for a big tub with jets.

I remember once touring the Vatican and St. Peter's,
Buildings resplendent in gold and art,
and every sort of precious decoration.

The women's rest room, however,
was a series of holes in the floor,
surrounded by dirty straw.
I said to myself, "the Pope can do better than this!"
Of course the Pope is unlikely to be in the Ladies' Room,
so maybe he is off the hook.

I'm glad I don't have that detail,
Or even a summer job at Disney
where inconsiderate tourists
make big messes, just taking a break.

Lord, some parts of life are just plain distasteful.
I wonder if Adam needed pooper scoopers;
I don't even want to think about conditions on the Ark
or in the Wilderness after the quails made everybody sick.

Nothing in Your world is without purpose, Lord,
not even bathroom duty.
The Apostle Paul calls himself a "fool for Christ,"
even calls himself
"the scum of the world, the refuse of all things."

Talk about an attack on our pride—
he really knows how to make the point!

I have heard that the Queen of England uses potty liners
made of kid leather.
Maybe so, but her bathroom still needs cleaning.

And so does mine, so I'd better get busy,
and enjoy my role as an unprofitable servant.

Sometimes we learn our lessons in the strangest places.

Tiring

If she coughs once more, Lord, I'll get up.
I promise
I love being a mom,
but I wonder if I'll ever catch up on my sleep.

The women in those cooey, gooey TV ads
never have bags under their eyes.
Their designer clothes provide a nice backdrop
for their spa makeup.
I suppose they have perfect children, too.
They never bundle up their little ones against the cold,
only to hear the sound of a diaper being filled to capacity
and have to start all over again.

I wonder what it was like to be Your mother.
Did you sleep through the night, unless disturbed
by shepherds or wise men?

I don't suppose You were ever sick.
I doubt You threw a tantrum at the bazaar,
or took Your siblings' toys
or picked Your nose in public.

The prophet Isaiah predicted
You would eat butter and honey.
I'll bet that was after You finished Your greens.

I wonder if You ever skinned your knee
or mashed Your thumb with Joseph's hammer.

I'll bet You were a good big brother
and a trustworthy helper around the house.

At the same time You were holding the universe together--
Now that's a mind boggling thought!

I'm glad You still have the cosmos in your hands,
and that You are ordering my world as well.

Thank you for the little one You have entrusted to me.
Already I need your help, and guidance, and strength.

If You could throw in a little time for a nap,
I'd really appreciate it!

Progressing

To her credit, she came to Bible Study, that day, Lord.
Without explanation
she had been ditched by her best friend.
They had shopped, chatted,
gone out to lunch,
shared meaningful scripture,
often prayed together.

Suddenly the calls were unanswered.
The sharing was over.
The newly mended heart re-broken.

That day we stayed after, talking
about David,
who lamented in Psalm 55,

If an enemy were insulting me,
  I could endure it;
if a foe were rising against me,
  I could hide.
But it is you, a man like myself,
  my companion, my close friend,
with whom I once enjoyed sweet fellowship
  at the house of God,
as we walked about
  among the worshipers.

We reminded ourselves
that You would bind up her broken heart
that You were the friend who sticks closer than a brother
that Your grace was sufficient

I feared someone so fragile as she
was ill equipped
to handle such a disappointment,
but You kept every one of those promises.

The last time I saw her she was thriving.

Forgive me for being surprised.

Rebuilding

I saw the blackbird in the park today, Lord.
Thank You that it is almost spring.
He is always the first, but soon robins
will be popping up everywhere.

I wonder if ours will ever return
(the ones that always build under the deck).
Last year the power washer
cruelly ripped away the nest
at just the time when little ones
were to pop their baby blue shells.

Helping with science homework, I learned a lot about birds.
First the male starts nests in several locations.
His mate is allowed to select the one she prefers.
Then she must finish the construction.

It's amazing the way You equip Your creatures
and use them for lessons
to teach us of Your care.

We know You see every sparrow that falls.
Were You saddened when our little robins were washed away?

In the Psalms many sparrows do find homes
and swallows build their nests near Your altars.
I can hardly fathom a God who thunders from Mt. Sinai
and yet is approachable by the tiniest of birds.

I relate a little more to the eagles of Deuteronomy
who push their young out of the nest,
so they can learn to fly.
Then they fly beneath the little ones
to avert disasters.

When my world is ripped apart,
And I search for the strength to rebuild one more time,
let it be near Your altars,
where I can rest in Your power and love.
As for flying,
I'm as reluctant as a host of baby eagles,
but I have no choice but to trust You.
Do I?

Trusting

Who will look after her, Lord?

I live so far away,
and my plane leaves in just a little while.

My stomach's upset at the thought.
Maybe I'm getting sick, too sick to travel!
Who am I kidding?
I know it's just nerves.

I wish she would wake up and encourage me through the goodbye. I remember that time I was struggling to leave.
I knew her heart was breaking, too, at having me go.
She pasted on a big smile and danced around.
"Spring is coming!" she shouted,
and waved until we drove out of sight.

Now she is in the winter of her life.
When I got the call, I thought she would see no more springs. Instead she has come out of the coma.
I'm so grateful, Lord, but I guess the ordeal has worn her out.
She mostly sleeps, waking only occasionally,
but she knows I have come.

I loved spending the night in her apartment,
surrounded by all that she is.
A grocery list in her precise writing lay on the table
until I tucked it in my purse.
Thank You for having it there.
I squeeze her hand in a last goodbye; she is sleeping again.

I think of the others who will look after her as best they can.
They have a lot on their plates already.
Please help them be able to do it all.

Forgive me for wanting to be here
when You have appointed me to other tasks.

Forgive me for crying out in my heart of hearts, "Oh, if only there were someone I could leave her with!"

I can't believe I just heard You say, clear as day,

"There is…"

Appreciating

I love the stanza of the old hymn, Lord:

… To our bountiful Father above,
We will offer our tribute of praise
For the glorious gift of His love
And the blessings that hallow our days.…

One of those blessings came my way today,
across the miles,
across the years:

A phone call from an old friend.
Who for ever so long had been
just a signature on a Christmas card.

Old friends always call on land lines
because that's the only number they have.
I was cleaning when the phone rang.
I figured it was another annoying junk call.

Instead, between the offer for long lasting light bulbs
and the suggestion I was being investigated by the IRS,
there came a truckload of memories--
a white truck, as she recalled,
in which we bumped down country lanes
while seeking little antique stores with bargain prices
and unusual wild flowers, blooming by the roadside.

I want to say we talked two hours,
although it was probably closer to three,

Laughing, catching up, rehashing our mutual history,
wondering what happened to the people we used to know,
and solving most of the world's current problems.

Thank you, Lord,
for hallowing my day
with all those remembered good times.

I am so undeserving
of the life I've been given,
Undeserving, but grateful.

Concurring

Lord, I absolutely love Your creation:
butterflies, and sunsets, and snowflakes (within reason, of course);
whippoorwills, and oceans, and fall maple trees;
Elephants, and peaches, and rocky mountains…

I could go on, but I might get around to cats,
greatly beloved by many, myself a possible exception.

Then there is your *pièce de ré·sis·tance*: the human race.
All those skin colors, and bone structures, and kinds of hair
and tones of voice, and hand shapes, and personalities.

I will have to say there was a time I didn't appreciate freckles
and big front teeth and cowlicks,
but those are minor inconveniences.

I'd just as soon our ears and noses didn't keep growing forever,
although I know it's Your way of amplifying our senses in old age.

As the Master of the Universe,
You obviously know what You are doing.

Lately, though, I have often thought I could use a third arm,
Like today, when I was trying to hang the blackout curtains
on an expansion rod between two window sills,
or just after visitors, while rolling up the spare mattress,
or when I have to set the grocery bags down to unlock the door.

I realize another appendage would greatly upset our symmetry
and make it way too easy to suck our thumbs into adulthood.

It would also be a deterrent to a garment's proper fit.
I have to hem the sleeves of every jacket I buy,
so there I'd be, stuck with another cuff to turn under.

Lord, I'm not complaining; it was just one of my crazy thoughts.

Please don't breathe a word about what I suggested.
I might be hailed by waving politicians
and ball catching athletes and bus drivers,
but I'd be blasted on *Facebook* by discus throwers and apron wearers
and weight watchers trying to firm up their guns.

Thank you that most of my body parts are still working.
In lieu of a third arm, big teeth come in really handy.

Prioritizing

I felt so sorry for my friend, Lord.

Her team blew a 21 point lead and lost by one.
She thought the players
were about to get their act together
and texted me, "I have hope."
Then the last basket rimmed out.

Tonight my team lost too.
I am trying to move on.

People are dying of AIDS.
Children are starving.
Crime is rampant.
Drugs are ruining lives.

Here we are, "good Christian people,"
worrying about Final Fours, and National Championships,
and Super Bowls, and World Series,
and a myriad of prize "Cups" for a variety of sports.

Games.
We have whole networks devoted to them.
At least four commentators
sit before the unfolding contests,
explaining what we can plainly see.

I have a neighbor whose TV
is divided into quarters,
so he can watch 4 games at once.

After a local team made the playoffs,
the church changed the date of an important meeting,
lest it be poorly attended.

What gives, Lord? Why do we love this stuff?

Why is our wardrobe packed with logo shirts and hats?

Why do we cheer on our teams every step of the way while our ministers beg for an "Amen"?

Sometimes I think our real church is a stadium,
where we go in hopes of being winners.

Too bad we don't realize that Jesus is the only game in town.

Surviving

What will they think of next?
A fair booth selling <u>organic</u> cotton candy?
I wonder if it's worth the extra dollar.

I gobble probiotics,
check the gluten content of our cereal.

I'm debating about vaccinating the children.
I'm on the Keto diet and eating non-GMO veggies.
I'm spinning and breathing deep
and checking my steps on my wrist.

All this is important, right?
Our bodies are temples of the Holy Spirit.
I know I read that somewhere, just before I started adding Kale to our salads.

Truth be told, the nutritional value
didn't seem to help at all
when I got on the treadmill.
It's funny that I go to the gym to use that machine.
Don't I live on something similar--
the job, the travel teams, diapers and prom dresses,
and we try hard to make it to church. We really do, Lord.

I look at this house.
There's even dust on the Bible.
That's a big no-no in all the devotional books.
Actually, I did try to squeeze in that evening study at church,
but it ended up being on the same night as Pilates.
Maybe when the kids go to college I'll have more time.

Well Lord, I have to get going. I'm sorry about the dusty Bible.
I promise to clean it off soon.
Meanwhile, I'd really appreciate if You would
keep the house from burning down this afternoon.
I'm putting the thin crust veggie pizza in the oven
before I drive the carpool home from Robotics.

Thanks. Lord, for being there when I need You.
You don't have to bother about the cotton candy.
I forgot we don't eat sugar.

Acquiescing

Life is full of irony, isn't it, Lord?

Take that story in the Bible about Elijah.

He prayed that it wouldn't rain in Israel.
Then he went to live by a brook.
The next thing you know, the brook dried up,
because he prayed it wouldn't rain.

I can relate.

I appealed to you for a better job for my husband.
Now he is too busy to do anything with the family.

I asked that my son make the team.
His homework is suffering.
I'm freezing in the bleachers and terrified he'll be injured.
I'm hoping the company he is keeping is on the up and up.

I prayed for companionship for my mother-in-law;
Now she lives in our guest room.

You allowed our daughter to make the cut
for the very best pre-school,
and we can barely afford it,
especially after we add art enrichment and dancing lessons
to keep up with her classmates.

I know Elijah was doing your will when he called off the rain.
Even so, he had to live with the outcome.

As for me, I'm not so sure I ended up with what I really wanted.
I remember that verse in Psalms that says,

"*And He gave them their request, but* sent leanness into *their soul.*"

Lord, I want Your will to be done
always
in my life.

The next time I ask for something
that may not be the best,
please say no.

I'd rather live with Your truth
than my consequences.

Interceding

I was amazed that a toddler could outrun me, Lord,
but he did have a head start,
waddling away from the playground
following a group walking away in the distance.

I wondered why they didn't wait,
until I realized he didn't belong with them at all.

Then the chase was on.
I managed to corral him long enough to point him
in the direction from which he had come.

When he squirted away again,
he wobbled dangerously close to the edge of the pond.

"Where is your Mama?" I asked.
When he didn't answer, and churned away,
I was astonished at the distance
those little legs could cover.

I lost him around the bend
and raced breathlessly ahead
and into the wooden enclosure.

Thank you for helping him find his mom.
When I approached the woman
who held his plump little body
just to let her know where he had been,

She greeted me with a look of agony,
saying over and over again,
"I'm sorry; I'm sorry; I'm so sorry."

I have an idea there was a lot more going on with her
than a little guy who temporarily misplaced himself.

I don't know what internal pain was so distracting.

You know, Lord.
I ask You to be
her Comfort, Guide, and Strength.

Please look after the little figure in the
knitted hat and the puffy coat
until she gets her act together.

Admiring

I want to be like her, Lord.

Managing a degree from a Christian college
in spite of dirt poverty.

Traveling to dark regions of the dark continent
to tell others about You,
Adopting unwanted children
and guiding the hands of lepers as they learn to write.

Retiring to the little house with the big garden.
so she could feast on the fruit of your abundance
and share the extras.

Reading the scripture
and books by those who wrote about You,
underlining in red, making notes,
typing inspirational passages
to mail to those who needed encouragement.

Worshipping in the familiar pew,
mostly misunderstood by family and the locals--
a prophet without honor in her own country.

When the dreaded days in the nursing home came,
she busied herself helping others more infirm,
cutting their meat at lunch
comforting them in the long, lonely days.

At last she lay in the infirmities of her age
confined to a room with two beds.

When at night her roommate cried out in fear,
she answered, "Don't be afraid; I'm here."
As at every other time, she would access Your grace
for You were ever by her side.

The tired old body was laid in a prepaid grave
in a small, obscure cemetery.

The spirit soared to her Savior's side.

The influence lives on
It has made me a better person
and reminds me still of Your goodness.

Hoping

A day at the museum—what fun, Lord.
Visiting them was a staple of my childhood.
Now I enjoy passing the habit to the next generation.

Although older itineraries featured oil paintings,
forts, and suits of armor,
today we can all be "hands on"
in miniature grocery stores with plastic oranges.
We can work as amateur carpenters
building houses with enormous blocks.

I love the helpful display of PVC pipe,
so that anyone can learn to install a drain,
and how about the water tables,
and the do it yourself puppet shows?

Recently we toured an institution where little folk
could climb and slide down a beanstalk
or ride in Cinderella's coach.

Another venue was adequately furnished with dinosaur bones,
and opportunities to creep through a tunnel avoiding a laser maze.

I enjoy visiting Your museum too, Lord,
where we meet the giants of the faith: Abel, Enoch, and Noah.

There's a room on Abraham and another on Moses,
with Isaac, Jacob, and Joseph sandwiched in between.

The display in the section featuring the Judges
is truly action packed:
trumpets, swords, foxes with fiery tails, the works.

Nearly all museums exit through the gift shops
for obvious reasons. Not Yours.
We are obliged to leave through the *Others* display.

There we learn of torture, mocking, flogging, chains, and prison.
People wander, hide, and suffer persecution.
In this life their faith is never rewarded.

Your museum is the most "true to life" of all.
Although I believe Your promise of "something better,"
Forgive me if I look for another exit on the way out.

Expecting

What was I thinking, Lord, when I said
I'd take over Women's Ministries for a year?

Without a budget, no less!

It was after that really great service.

I was still in praise mode, and the pastor caught me off guard.

I'd have promised anything,

I can relate to Peter, blundering out of the boat
after seeing You walking toward him on the sea,
But now, talk about getting cold feet,
I can just feel the waves
lapping around my ankles

You know how it is: everybody brings
the same sweet potato casserole
to the covered dish lunches.

Then there's the woman
who goes on and on about her aunt's infected toe
when we're trying to start the program.

Program? What program? Did I mention there's no budget?

Maybe we could make turkeys out of pine cones and discuss being
thankful, but that's only going to work once.

Should we do a Bible study and start with Genesis?

We could talk about your blowing
on a pile of dust and making it a living soul.

That must have been quite a breath.

Oh Lord, are you trying to tell me something?

Maybe I just need to take a deep breath
and let You come up with the ideas.
Maybe You'll help me bubble back to the surface
and keep my head above water.

Did I say maybe? That's no way to talk
to the Lord of the Universe, is it?

If You will blow some life into this ministry,
I'm ready to go look for pine cones.

Despairing

Lord, what have we done to our world
to make our young despair of life
so quickly?

Too often the obituary page
offers the sad information:
"passed away suddenly at home."

Is it the pop culture that sets the example,
when the rich and famous icons of our day
choose to be embraced by the shadowy arms of death?

Is it our broken homes, our minds skewed on drugs,
the violence surrounding us, the too great expectations
that exceed all abilities to perform?

When I search Your word for answers,
I see men of old
taking their mortality into their own hands.

Abimelech, Samson, Saul and his armor bearer,
Ahithophel, Zimri,
and, of course, Judas.

Each one, it seems, sought the ultimate despair
when shame ruled out any spark of hope.

Each could not bear to face the guilt
of poor decisions that led to an unbearable defeat.

Each had lost a battle for significance by courting sin.

Lord, just as You relate the stories of Israel
to teach us lessons,
enlighten us by the mistakes of these men.

Show us, and especially our children,
that You are the One who makes us significant,
that You nailed all our shame on Calvary's tree.

We read that You Yourself
"sorrowed unto death" in Gethsemane.
You understood the dark tunnel of hopelessness.
You despised the shame of the cross,
but endured it
For us!

Remembering

When the car wound up the mountain road that crisp fall morning, it
was outstripped by my soaring spirit,
anticipating a day at the top of the world.

The sky was October blue,
a perfect backdrop for the colorful trees
that held out leafy hands in salute.

The air was clear and just crisp enough
to be cooling after a hike to the falls.

Little ponies in a hillside pen seemed to toss their tails with glee.

The lady selling honey was all smiles as she waved,
hoping to sell her jars of sweetness,

But I was in a hurry to get to the top, where the stew was bubbling
and people were shuffling through the leaves to make selections from
paintings hanging on clothes lines. Wood carvers danced little men on
paddles. Potters offered original cereal bowls. Someone was selling old
books. I tore myself away for a breathless view of the canyon, but not
until I bought a painted rock—now there was an idea I could copy.

Jesus, when you were born, Mary stored many things in her heart:
angels, shepherds, worshipping Magi and the like.
I don't have that kind of resume by a long shot, but You gave me ever
so many things to ponder on that sparkling, joyous day:

The wind tossing my hair, fragrant with wood smoke.
The fun of commandeering a sturdy stick
for help climbing the rocks.
The delight of feasting on the view of Your creation
in the valley below.
I was as full of life as the bouncing man on the carver's paddle.

But even then, I knew there would come a day
when the valley wouldn't seem so pleasant.
I would feel trapped there by insurmountable, barren peaks.

At such times, Lord, remind me to warm myself
by the golden memory of that perfect fall day,
when my friend and I sang
as we drove down the mountain
and reflected on Your goodness

Valuing

Patience in tribulation—he personified that, Lord,
as he lived out every lesson he tried to teach us.

Once he was full of life,
working hard to provide,
refusing us the luxury of being lazy,
loving a good joke--

He told us the big hole in the back yard
was going to be a bomb shelter,
until we suddenly realized
it was a swimming pool.
He finished our basement
before most people thought
about building rec rooms.

He took us to the beach in summer,
(rescued us when our inner tubes overturned,)
taught us to love travel, and people, and country, and God.

By the time he was a grandfather,
he was ready to do it all again,
except he had been felled by disease
and could only stumble behind the stroller,
pushing it up and down the driveway.

He rarely complained,
even on the darkest day of his life
when he left home for years of nursing care.

He made friends with the caregivers,
maybe even with the hallucinations
caused by his meds.

He didn't ask for much:
a jar of figs, if you were going to the store,
or maybe a box of odds and ends,
so he could see what he could make.

Lord, I pray I may fight the good fight
half as well as he did.
Thank You for a tangible example
of a good and faithful servant.

Cleaning

Clutter! Oh my goodness, Lord.
It's a never-ending battle.

I toss, toss, toss, but it's really the old scrapbooks
and photo albums that take up so much space.

I've ripped signed pages from yearbooks
and designated the remains for landfills.
I've held yard sales and dealt with antique dealers,
given to newlyweds and ministry thrift shops.
My scanner files are replete with old documents and clippings.

I know I don't need my newspaper picture
of the high school honor society
or the little drawing of Mickey Mouse
our oldest drew on a trip to Disney.

Diamonds and pearls I can live without,
but memories,
they are so hard to discard.

I read in Ephesians that You emptied Yourself
before You came to our world in the flesh--
the Lord of glory, reduced to servant status.
What an amazing act of love and sacrifice!

On earth, You had no place to lay Your head
and traveled in the clothes on your back.
Was that ultimate freedom, Lord?

Didn't You ever wish you had a place to keep
Joseph's well-worn hammer
or the remnants of a threadbare scroll
You brought home from the Temple at twelve?

I can't help imagining Mary treasuring
a little box of swaddling clothes.
Instead, she just remembered.

I'm not there yet, Lord.
Help me loosen my hold on the past
in anticipation of Your future goodness.

Tolerating

Lord, I remember Job got into big trouble
raising questions he had no business asking,
though who could blame him?
Most of us certainly aren't in his ball park.

Being finite and sinful,
we all have our list
of explanations we can't wait to hear
when we come to be with You.

Somehow I won't be in a hurry to learn
Your thoughts on the 5 points of Calvinism,
and the preferred form of baptism,
and the endurance of spiritual gifts.

It's about those little foxes that spoil the grapes:
I wonder why Noah didn't step on the cockroaches
and swat at the mosquitoes when they tried to get on board.

I know everything must have been made with a purpose,
even those,
but Telemarketers? Seriously?

Our phone rings off the hook
and our voicemails overflow.
Our devices choke on spam.

Today in a store I was twice accosted
by folks with internet deals
and big savings on my electric bill;
that's only because the thermal window salesman
was on a lunch break.

Lord, I understand these people
are trying to make a living,
and I am certainly no better than they,
but, often, before I think
I treat them with less grace than I'd have
for a snarling dog.

The old translation of the scripture exhorts:
let us go on to perfection.
Whenever I think I'm making a little progress,
the phone rings, and I know I still have a long way to go.

Constructing

Lord, it didn't look that difficult,
just to make a doll for a baby gift.
No, I didn't know how to sew,
but how hard could it be?

I guess I forgot my attempts from years past:
the blouse with the ragged facing,
the slacks that required the wearer
to walk like a hobbled prisoner,
the one zipper I replaced badly.

At first it was smooth sailing;
then came the legs.
By the time I assembled
all body parts correctly,
I was not the least bit enthusiastic
about setting in tiny sleeves,
and gathering the waist of lacy bloomers.

Finally, all I had to do
was embroider a name on the hem of her skirt,
one that would make her unique.

I wonder, Lord, was molding our bodies
the easy job?
We are still trying to understand
the way You made our inmost parts.

We measure ourselves on the Enneagram
and again on the Myers-Briggs.

We analyze our love languages,
and compare our leadership styles
to doves, owls, peacocks, and eagles.

We sort through pages of scripture
to discern spiritual gifts,
and identify as sanguine, choleric,
melancholic, or phlegmatic.

Whatever my category,
You wired me to take a creative risk,
but, more important,
You took a risk on making me.

Welcoming

You know what I miss, Lord?
Front porches.

Houses used to have them,
places where gliders squeaked,
or swings hung by chains.

Usually there were a couple of rockers,
and, sometimes, one of those springy,
cloth baby seats that hung from the ceiling.

Porches were places to relax,
wave to neighbors,
watch games of stickball
and hopscotch.

All grandparents seemed to have porches,
with a history of snapped beans,
and hand held fans,
and, in winter,
a snowman standing sentinel in the yard.

Now we go out back,
grill on our decks,
and rush inside to climate control.

After all, the tournament's on,
as is the *X-Box*,
practice starts soon,
and it's time for a conference call
from another time zone.

Lord, I confess:
we only have a deck.
Even so, grant me today
a front porch mentality,
of relaxing and enjoying
little things, simple things,
and real people, not images on a screen.

Give me the compassion of a grandparent
rushing to the aid of a toddler who scraped a knee
and needs a little bit of rocking.

Providing

Temptations come in all sorts of venues, don't they, Lord?
You know the kitchen is not my favorite place,
and the grocery store is first runner up.

I've tried to improve my attitude in various ways:
the "people are starving" guilt routine;
the Brother Lawrence idea of making every chore an act of service;
the gratitude for hungry mouths to feed.

Nothing works very well.
Anyway, here I am; it's meal planning time.
I have ingredients for any number of options,
dishes that require thawing, browning, chopping, mixing…
the word for that is *trouble*, Lord.

My afternoon preferences lie in other activities,
some useful; some, I admit, a little selfish.
I really want to grab cooked slices at the ham store.
(Serve at room temperature.)
The farm market sells great pulled pork.
(Add sauce and warm in the oven.)

I rack my brain for scriptures about the great conflict:
ham versus swiss steak, or oven chicken, or meatloaf.

Immediately I think of the virtuous woman in Proverbs 31:

She is like the merchant ships,
   bringing her food from afar
She gets up while it is still night;
   she provides food for her family.

I'm afraid I'm still confused.
It sounds as if she goes to the ham store
after rising at dawn to make yeast rolls.

OK, Lord, I'll thaw some chicken for a casserole.
The big question now is whether to watch HGTV
or listen to a book on tape while I work.

Just don't expect me to whistle.

Empathizing

I know we'll be OK, Lord.
There are other jobs,
and he got a nice package
that will tide us over.

It's not so much a financial blow,
but a real shock to his self-worth.

I know these acquisitions happen all the time.
He survived the first few.
Now he has been ungraciously replaced
by a young modern with a degree
from a fancy college and "connections."

It's hard to see someone
put on the shelf,
when he's at the top of his game,
still brimming with untried ideas,
still having so much to offer.

Last Sunday was a nightmare.
I know the pastor meant well
when he asked people to stand
who needed jobs.
What an embarrassment to be relegated
to the ranks of the unuseful!

I think of the parable of the laborers
who worked for different amounts of time,
yet were all given the same pay.
Unfair? Not quite.
Those who came early to the field
were given the dignity
of being chosen, wanted.

The workers hired last
endured the stares that marked them as
lazy, second rate, undesirable, over the hill.
They would have welcomed the heat of the day.

Some of us are designed to want more
than a trip to the gym
or a day at the golf course.
Lord, be kind to my diligent breadwinner,
waiting for his hire.

Searching

Where did I put it, Lord?

You know, the present I bought in January and now need to mail.

I've looked in the gift chest, the spare room closet, the trunk...
It just has to be one of those places, but it's not.
I remember putting it in that cute box
I wasn't sure I wanted to part with.

Come on, Lord! <u>You</u> know where it is!

You also know I often forget where I put things.
Do I get points for planning ahead and shopping economically,
or just a slew of demerits for a cluttered brain?

You are perfectly willing to let me stew in my own juice even when I have a tight schedule? And it's for my good, right?

I remember those parables You told: the lady who lost the coin, the shepherd seeking his sheep, and the father welcoming his runaway son back into the fold.

I get the rejoicing part, because I'd sure like to find that gift. Even so, I think You are saying something more with those stories.

We can easily become frantic when something is mislaid, yet all our little struggles are trivia compared to Yours.

You are the Desperate Seeker, and the stakes are higher.
Like the searchers in the parables, You look; You pursue; You wait.
When the lost one is restored, You rejoice like a Superbowl champ, and all heaven with You.

From now on, when I'm rambling through closets and drawers, I'm going to try to be grateful in my frustration—thankful that You cared enough to search for me when I was lost.

Even if I don't find what I'm looking for,
I'm awfully glad you found me.
Thank You for using my exasperation
to teach me a lesson.
I wouldn't mind a tiny little hint, though,
if it wouldn't interfere with my spiritual growth.

Embarking

Did you miss me, Lord?

We were out of here yesterday
at the crack of dawn,
traveling some distance
to launch our eldest
in the next chapter of life.

What an exciting time!
We were so thrilled
for the new opportunities.

It seems we had just put away the crib,
gotten the braces,
taken the SAT's,
insisted on the part time job.

Now we were on the launch pad
of a new adventure,
lugging boxes up the stairs,
hanging clothes in a different closet,
acclimating to a new venue,
greeting a host of people
with unknown faces.

The goodbyes weren't as hard
as I thought they might be,
though most of the family had
misty eyed smiles.

Not me. I was strong,
until we reached the house
and saw the empty parking place
in the driveway.

This isn't going to be easy, Lord.
I'm beginning
a new chapter in my life as well.

Please help me through Day One.

Part II: Meditation

Ever been between
"a rock and a hard place"?
Jesus turned down the temptation
to change the rock into bread
and turned instead to the scripture.

In the space provided
translate each of the scripture ideas
that follow
into a thought for the day.

Beginning
Luke 10:38-42

Spending
Genesis 28:20-22; II Corinthians 9: 6-7; Galatians 6:7

Reading
Joshua 1:8; Psalms 119:105; Proverbs 4:1-13; Romans 15:4

Singing
II Chronicles 5:11-14; Psalm 98:1; Colossians 3:16

Rebooting
Luke 2:52; Philippians 3:10-14

Persevering
Matthew 24: 22; Malachi 4:2; Job 19:25

Respecting
Ephesians 4:32; I Thessalonians 5:15; II Peter 1:5-8

Enduring
Matthew 11:28-29; Exodus 33:14; Isaiah 26:2-4

Adjusting
Genesis 12:1; Hebrews 13:14; John 14:2;
Deuteronomy 31:8

Redeeming
John 2: 1-11; Mark 2:16-17; I Corinthians 10:31;
Ephesians 5:16

Encouraging
Deuteronomy 33:27; Philippians 4:7; Matthew 9:20-22;
Isaiah 40:31

Missing
Genesis 1:24-25; Proverbs 17:17; John 15:12; I Peter 4:8

Accepting
Romans 5:8; Romans 15:1; Colossians 3: 12-14;
Hebrews 10:24; I Peter 3:8

Stressing
Psalms 37:7; Jeremiah 29:11; Philippians 4:6

Caring
Galatians 6:1-2; Philippians 2:4; I Thessalonians 5:11

Serving
I Corinthians 4: 1-2; Luke 17: 7-10; John 13: 1-17

Tiring
Exodus 33:14; Isaiah 7:15; Isaiah 40:29; Galatians 6:9; Philippians 4:13;
I Thessalonians 2:7

Progressing
Psalm 55:12-14; Proverbs 18:24; Isaiah 61:1;
II Corinthians 12:9

Rebuilding
Deuteronomy 32:11; Psalm 84:3-4; Matthew 10:29-31; Isaiah 40:31

Trusting
Psalm 71:5; Psalm 86:17; Psalm 119:76; Isaiah 49:13; Lamentations 3:25; John 14:27

Appreciating
Proverbs 27:9; Ecclesiastes 4:9-10; James 1:17; Matthew 8:20; I John 4:7

Concurring
Job 22: 21-22; Isaiah 29:16; Isaiah 45:9; Acts 4:24; Romans 9:20-21; Revelation 5:13-14

Prioritizing
Psalm 90:12; Micah 6:8; Matthew 6:33; Luke 12:34

Surviving
Psalm 37:5; Psalm 46:10; Matthew 11:28; Luke 8:14; I John 2:17

Acquiescing

I Kings 17:1-7; Psalms 106 15; James 3: 17-18

Interceding

I Samuel 12:23: Lamentations 3: 48-50; Romans 8:26;
I Timothy 2:1; Hebrews 7:25; James 5:17

Admiring

Matthew 13:57; Galatians 6:1-4; Hebrews 10:24;
John 13:34; Psalm 116:15

Hoping

Hebrews 11

Expecting

Genesis 2:7; Matthew 14: 22-33; James 1:5

Despairing

Judges 9:54; Judges 16:30; I Samuel 31:4-5; II Samuel 17:23; I Kings 16:18; Matthew 27:5; Matthew 26:38; Hebrews 12:2

Remembering

Luke 2:19; Psalm 121:1-2; Isaiah 40: 1-5; Isaiah 46: 8-10;
I Timothy 6:17

Valuing
Romans 12:12; II Timothy 2: 3-4; II Timothy 4: 7-8;
Matthew 25:23

Cleaning
Psalm 23:6; Matthew 6:19-21; Matthew 8:20;
Luke 2:18-20; Philippians 2:5-8

Tolerating
Genesis 7:1-5; Job:31; Job 38-41; Proverbs 16:4;
Song of Solomon 2:15; Hebrews 6:1

Constructing
Psalm 139:13-14; Romans 12:6-8;
I Corinthians 12: 4-11; Ephesians 4:11-12; I Peter 4:10-11

Welcoming
Leviticus 19:33-3; Luke 14:12-14; Matthew 25:34-40; Romans 12: 13-16; Hebrews 13:2; I Peter 4: 8-9

Providing
Proverbs 30:24-25; Proverbs 31:14-15; John 21:1-14;
I Corinthians 10:31

Empathizing
Matthew 20:1-16

Searching
Luke 15:1-32

Embarking
Psalm 119: 105; Proverbs 3:5-6; Proverbs 4:18
Proverbs 22:6; Jeremiah 29:11

Part III: Application

Got questions?
Don't we all.

Try answering the practical questions
that follow in the space provided.
There is not necessarily one "right answer."

Beginning

Imagine that a prominent religious leader and twelve of his closest friends have decided to join your family for dinner. Describe your plan to show the hospitality they deserve and still benefit from their visit.

Spending

In Genesis 28 Jacob makes God a business proposal of sorts. Does it seem to be a good idea?

How hard is it to be a cheerful giver?

Some ministries stress "the law of the harvest," sowing in order to reap. Does this practice emphasize the cause or the result? Should this principle be a guide for giving?

Singing and Reading

Some music is obviously designed for worship. What about the rest of it?

Skim through Genesis 4 to discover the originator of music, as far as the scripture is concerned. Why might the answer seem a bit surprising?

Why is it easier to read part of a good novel than a chapter in the Bible?

So many books, so little time—how do we choose our reading material?

In the light of John 1:1 is the Bible different from other books, even other religious books? Why or why not?

Rebooting

Is it easier to be in favor with God or with people? Why?

Paul tells us his goal and his plans for reaching it. Do his ideas work "in the real world"?

What are some positive ways to express frustration with others?

Respecting

How can we disagree respectfully with people who don't share our point of view?

Are freedom of speech and respect mutually exclusive?

How do we know which people God has on our list?

Persevering

Some people flee to warmer climes during the gloom of winter. Is it possible to flee emotional gloom in a similar way? How would such a strategy look?

We have a name for people being trapped in perpetual emotional darkness. Depression is a major problem in our culture. What parts of modern life drag us into this uncomfortable illness?

How might a person cope who works the night shift or mines coal in the depths of the earth?

Enduring

In dealing with one another's failures, what is the best way to balance forgiveness and tough love?

How can families come together when there is disagreement over important issues that affect each member?

What is a good strategy for self-care important during stressful times?

Adjusting

Why is change of any kind difficult?

What make the *status quo* so comfortable?

Is it true that "every cloud has a silver lining"?

Redeeming

What, in particular, makes situations dull, uncomfortable, or distasteful for us?

What advance strategies might help mitigate our discomfort in seemingly negative circumstances?

How can we shift our focus from ourselves to others?

Encouraging

What are at least three ways we can encourage friends who are enduring hardships?

Some people choose to withdraw in times of trouble. How can we both respect their privacy and be supportive?

God always keeps His promises, but sometimes scriptures seem to be meaningless platitudes in times of crisis. How can we offer His word in meaningful ways?

Missing

Some people today are choosing to have pets instead of children. Shops on every corner offer a variety of products from rhinestone collars to strollers for aging animals. Comment on this phenomenon as an observation on our society.

Many people today are passionate about adopting unfortunate animals while foster children languish within the system. Is one choice better than the other.? Why or why not?

What lesson does the ownership of animals teach us about friendship?

Accepting

Gender Identify seems to be a staple of modern life. What has created the problems associated with this issue?

Prepare in advance a comment you might make to a person struggling with gender dysphoria, if you were asked for an opinion on this matter, what would you say?

No matter how we might choose to help such a struggler, are there non-negotiables in our opinions?

Stressing

When we have to "wait on the Lord," is our discomfort caused by a need for instant gratification or something else?

From a heavenly standpoint why might God "wait" to answer a prayer?

Are there prayers that God will always answer immediately?

Caring

Are there such things as divine appointments?

What is the best way to help someone who doesn't heed wise counsel?

How do we respond to advice that others speak into our lives?

Serving

What is the best way to accomplish thankless or distasteful tasks?

Would an ideal life consist of having countless servants to free our lives for full time enjoyment?

What emotions might Jesus have experienced while washing the disciples' dirty feet?

Tiring

What practical strategies might help a person plan for tiring situations?

How does the way we care for our children teach us about the love of a Heavenly Father?

Job 35:10 tells us our Maker gives us songs in the night. How do we access these when we are facing a literal or figurative night of unrest?

Progressing

What purposes do friendships serve?

What is a good balance between privacy and transparency in a friendship?

What determines our willingness to share ourselves with others?

Rebuilding

Sometimes we encounter persistent spiders who spin their webs across our doors, no matter how many times these are destroyed. The scripture suggests we forgive someone seventy times seven. Do the same statistics apply to rebuilding?

What sorts of issues are worthy of repeated attempts at repairing?

How do we determine that further rebuilding is not a viable option?

Trusting

Is there really another option to trusting God for the issues of life?

How does trusting God promote peace within ourselves?

In choosing trust over worry, how do we simplify our lives?

Appreciating

Explain ways to cultivate a habit of appreciation.

How should we apply the old saying: "We don't miss the water until the well runs dry."

a. by appreciating the water

b. by planning for a dry well

c. by living in the moment

Is it possible that negative, as well as positive events can hallow our days?

Concurring

How many of us are completely satisfied with the way God made us?

To what extent should we attempt to alter our basic appearance or design?

"Shaming" has become a media phenomenon in our culture. How can we eradicate its negative effects on ourselves or others?

Prioritizing

Why are many of us obsessed with sporting events?

How do we help our children balance the demands of the youth group and the travel team?

For the Christian, what is "sportsmanlike conduct?"

Surviving

How do we know which messages regarding our health and welfare to believe?

Is a hugely busy lifestyle really necessary?

How can we order our lives to include serenity with other beneficial activities in our lives?

Acquiescing

What sometimes motivates our struggle with "best things"?

What skews our ability to know what "best things" are?

Is there a rule of thumb for balancing aspirations with biblical values?

Interceding

What are some ways we can make a difference in the lives of complete strangers?

What are some ways we can make a difference in the lives of "nodding acquaintances"?

What are some ways we can make a difference in the lives of those closest to us?

Which of these choices is hardest?

Admiring

How is it possible to serve the Lord actively until we draw our last breath?

In some cultures the elderly are revered; in others they are considered a nuisance. If we someday fall into the latter category, how can we continue to live a purposeful life?

John Milton, author of *Paradise Lost*, lost his eyesight in the midst of a productive writing career. In a sonnet about this affliction, he penned the words, "He also serves who only stands and waits." What did he mean?

Hoping

Why are the latter verses of Hebrews 11 unsettling?

At the same time, why are these verses helpful?

Does it take more faith to face a giant, risk a lion's den, or simply stand for one's beliefs?

How does a person stock up on faith, just in case?

Remembering

How can we give ourselves completely to the mountaintop experience knowing that it won't last?

In Matthew 17: 1-2 Jesus is on a mountain with three of his disciples. Are there lessons in this passage about mountaintop experiences?

Drug users talk about getting "high." How are they trying to simulate experiences we all crave?

Which seems more appealing: a life with highs and lows or a flatline, predictable existence?

Valuing

An old hymn begins: "Am I a soldier of the cross…?" What does it mean to be a soldier of the cross?

What resources does a Christian have for being "patient in tribulation?"

What purpose do people serve who doze all day in the halls of care facilities?

Cleaning

Why do we save the preschool papers and press the flowers from a prom bouquet? Or--Why do we discard them?

What makes some of our holidays rather nostalgic?

People who live in convents or monastic orders sometimes have only a bare room and a few necessities. Does this lifestyle represent the ultimate freedom?

Tolerating

Sponsors of nuisance invasions of our privacy pay people to contact us with their message. Are these tactics sometimes productive? Why?

As Jesus walked from place to place, he was often accosted by those who wanted his help. In Matthew 15: 21-28 a woman's persistence won the day. Why did Jesus ultimately give her his attention?

Why do we resent "junk" calls and aggressive sales people?

Constructing

Is it true that opposites attract, or do we gravitate toward people who are like ourselves?

Is it a good idea to find our personal category in the scheme of things, or does that kind of knowledge matter?

Some people enjoy standing out in a crowd and others shy away from being unique. What are some possible reasons for these reactions?

Welcoming

Stranger support GoFundMe requests and "like" posts on *Facebook*. Are these responses the modern version of the "front porch" lifestyle?

Have decks replaced front porches for aesthetic reasons, or do they represent a move away from community?

Some businesses have eliminated cubicles or offices and have all employee workstations in one big room? Good idea? Why or why not?

Providing

Do hand peeled, boiled, and manually whipped potatoes reflect godliness more than the add boiling water, instant variety?

Barring physical pain, grief, and other heavy duty emotional issues, is it possible to find enjoyment in mundane tasks?

Did Jesus mind sweeping the carpenter shop?

Empathizing

How can we support someone who is struggling with feelings of self-worth?

What accounts for our differing ideas about work?

During the Great Depression's massive unemployment, the crime rate was actually low. What might be the reason for this unusual statistic?

Searching

What emotions are involved in searching for something that has been mislaid?

What exactly does the scripture mean in regard Christ coming "to seek and save the lost." Doesn't an all-knowing God know where we are?

How do we decide when to "give up" on a search? Does God have a timetable for "giving up" on a person?

Embarking

What are some life events that require a new beginning?

What are some life events that involve "letting go"?

What are some strategies for surviving these events joyfully?

*This is not the end,
only the beginning:
it's time for Marthas everywhere
to write their own book of prayers.*

www.ingramcontent.com/pod-product-compliance
Lightning Source LLC
Chambersburg PA
CBHW050203130526
44591CB00034B/2041